B

Letters

PLAY BAC
PUBLISHING
More.Brain.Power

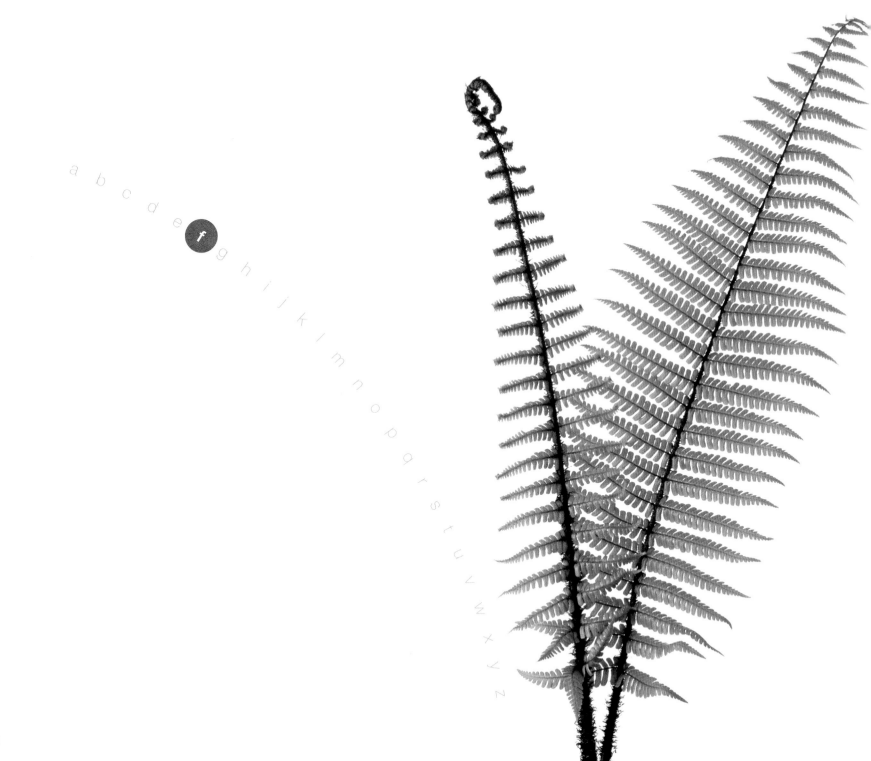

a b c d e **f** g h i j k l m n o p q r s t u v w x y z

Follow an inviting new path to learning the alphabet.

Bright and bold colors and characters make letters leap from the page and into the imagination. Plants, animals, and landscapes create the perfect atmosphere for learning. Will the turtle ever reach the tulips? Do parrots really eat peas?

What do the cat and the caterpillar have in common, besides the letter "C"?

Take a closer look at the alphabet and you will find that nature is an excellent teacher!

Let's start things off right:
I'd like to take a bite!
The apple is so tempting –
Red and round, it's just the thing.

The alligator says, "That apple's got some shine!"
You may have it, but the avocado's all mine!

A

apple

a b c d e f g

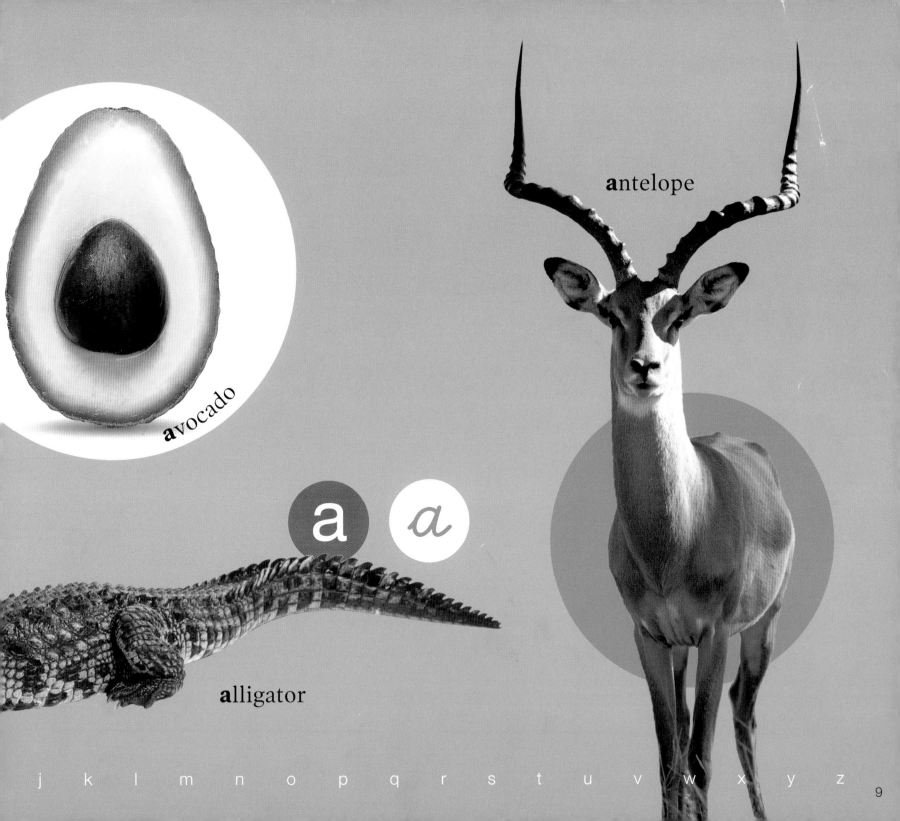

avocado

antelope

a a

alligator

B

buffalo

a b c d e f g h i j k l m n o p q r s t u v w x y z

Buffalo, Buffalo
What do you see?
My badger friend, a ripe banana,
and some bright broccoli!

Bravo!
You know
What's good for you:
Banana and broccoli
Just like the buffalo and the badger do!

banana

broccoli

badger

11

carrots

caterpillar

crab

a b c d e f g h i j k l m n o p q r s t u v w x y z

C

12

C

cat

Cat sees the cherries and dreams of a cherry ice cream float.
Caterpillar likes his stripes and wonders, "Where'd you get your coat?"

The caterpillar and the cat have matching striped suits.
"I don't mind," says the crab.
"I'd rather eat the fruits."

cherries

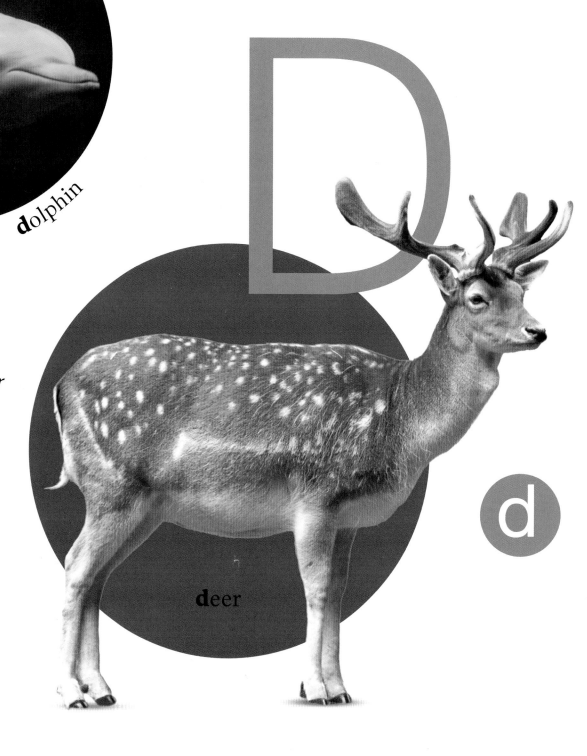

dolphin

D d

deer

The dolphin and the deer
Steer clear of the dune.
The dahlia, so pretty,
looks like a pink balloon.

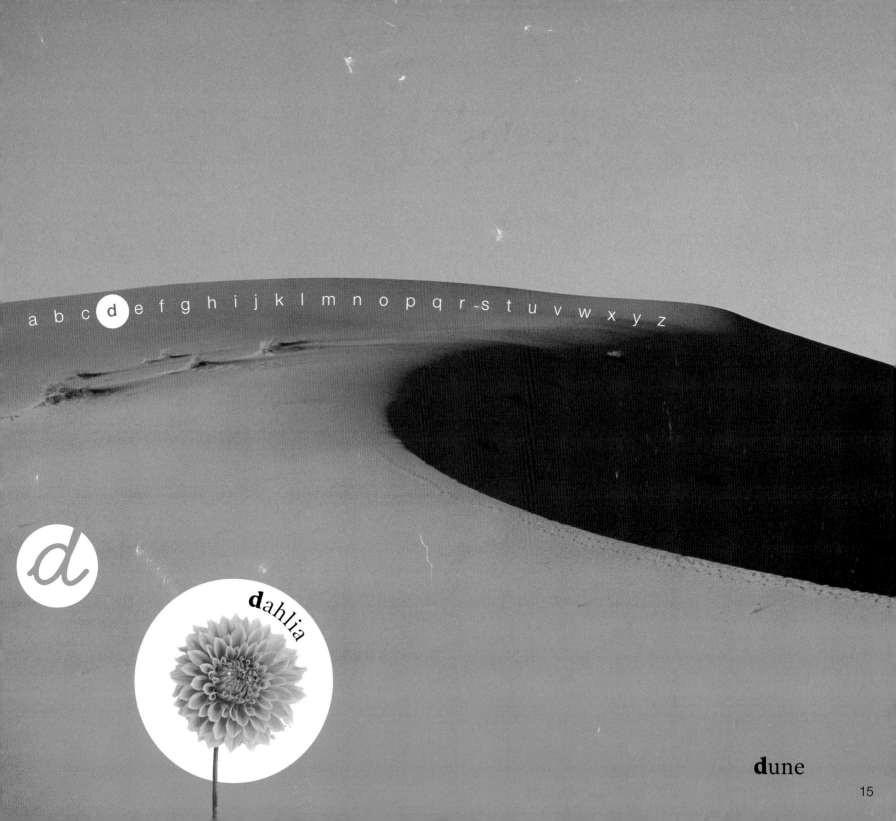

a b c **d** e f g h i j k l m n o p q r s t u v w x y z

dahlia

dune

15

Endive or corn?
The elephant toots his horn,
"I like mine popped:
Corn that way just can't be topped!"

endive

i j k l m n o p q r s t u v w x y z

elephant

ears of corn

f f

figs

I'm foraging in the ferns,
Waiting for the flamingos to take their turns.
I just hope they don't get sunburns.

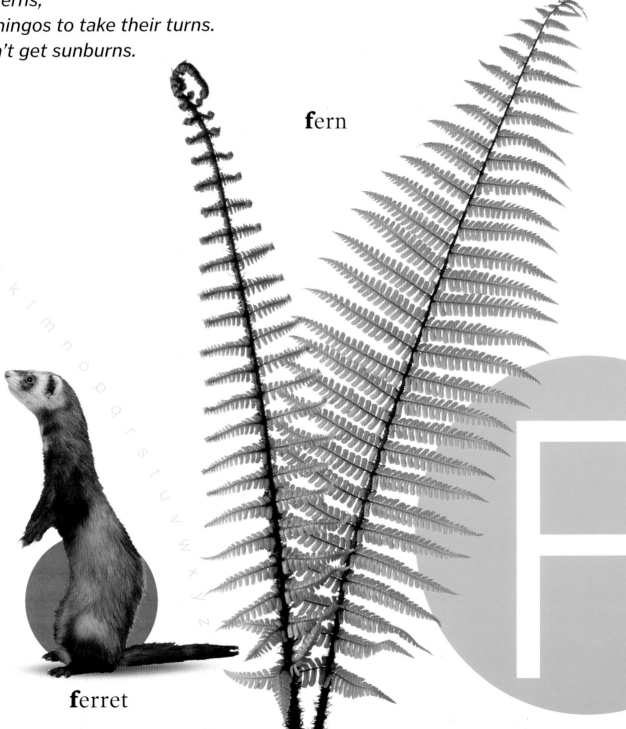

fern

ferret

gull

g g

grapes

gorilla

Toss me a grape!
The giraffe's trying to escape!
Easy now, no need to go ape!

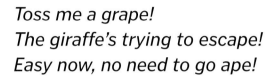

ginkgo

giraffes

hippopotamus

The hamster spies the holly.
"It makes me feel so jolly!"
The hippo is distracted, dreaming
of a hot tamale.

h   *h*

hydrangea

hamster

holly

a b c d e f g **h** i j k l m n o p q r s t u v w x y z

iguana

The iguana imagines an igloo.
To keep warm, there isn't much
he wouldn't do.
He would prefer the island.
The impala says, "Me too!"

iceberg

island

I

i i

impala

J

j j

jellyfish

jaguar

a b c d e f g h i j k l m n o p q r s t u v w x y z

26

jack fruit

Would a jaguar eat a jellyfish?
I don't think so, it's not his dish.
He likes food that doesn't go "squish!"

Jack Russell terriers

koala

K

a b c d e f g h i j **k** l m n

kiwis

q r s t u v w x y z

k

k

*The cuddly koala perches in a tree.
The kiwi eyes a different kiwi,
While kangaroo keeps baby under
lock and key.*

kangaroo

kiwi

lion

lavender

a b c d

30

g h i j k l m n o p q r s t u v w x y z

The lizard circles to get a better view
Of the lily and the lavender;
The lion says "ah-choo!"

lizard

L *l*

lily

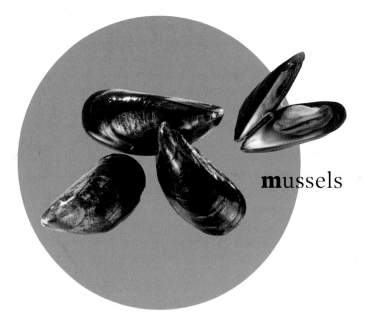

mussels

M

Mango and mussels
I love to eat.
Meet me on the mountain
for a picnic treat!

mango

mongoose

a b c d e f g h i j k l **m** n o p q r s t u v w x y z

mountain

I've feathered my nest, and dinner is ready:
Nectarines and nuts,
But I prefer spaghetti.

N

nest

nuts

nightingale

nasturtium

nectarine

a b c d e f g h i j k l m **n** o p q r s t u v w x y z

n *n*

35

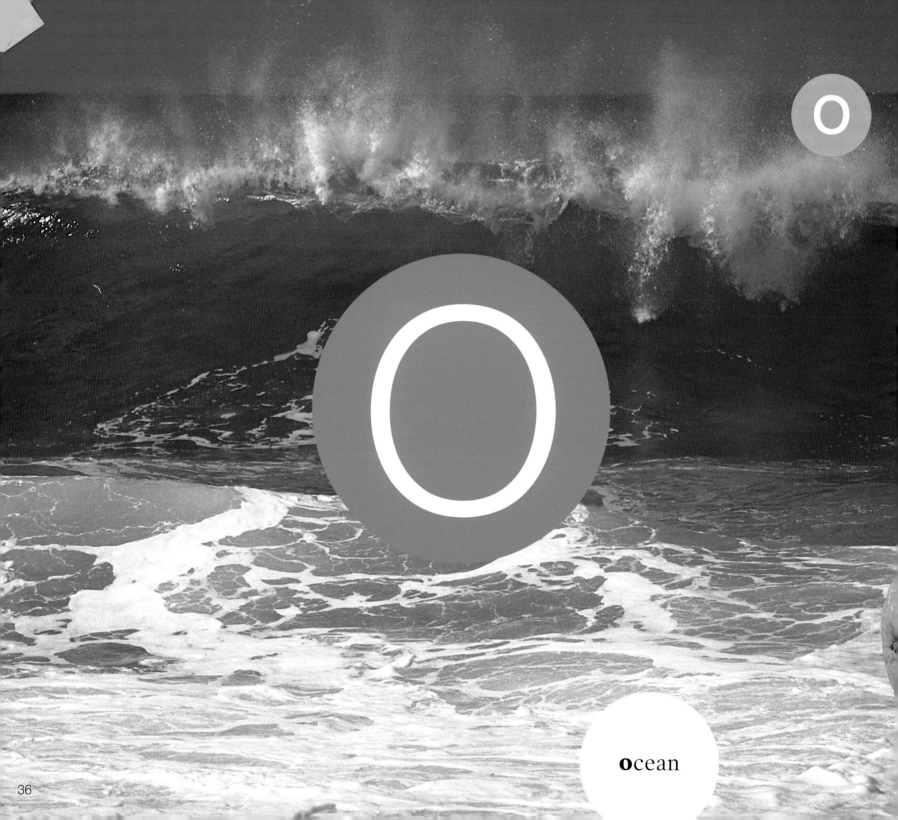

O

ocean

The "O" is round
Like the orange on the ground.
The opossum and orangutan do
not make a sound -
They wish they were going to
the playground.

orange

opossum

orangutan

P

peas

parrot

a b c d e f g h i j k l m n o **p** q r s t u v w x y z

38

These are my peas!
These are my peas!
"Don't repeat yourself," said the pony.
"I'd rather eat cheese."

pear

pumpkin

pony

Q q

quetzal

quartz

Q

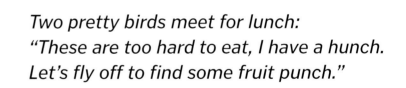

Two pretty birds meet for lunch:
"These are too hard to eat, I have a hunch.
Let's fly off to find some fruit punch."

quahogs

quail

r r

radish

rhinoceros

rose

R

ray

We're rushing for radishes, you see.
I run over land,
I fly through the sea,
Let's rush, rush, rush!
Our radishes are ready!

raccoon

snake

sand

S

a b c d e f g h i j k l m n o p q r s t u v w x y z

S s

squirrel

salt

salamander**s**

Salt and pepper?
No, salt and sand.
Don't make that mistake
At the hot-dog stand!

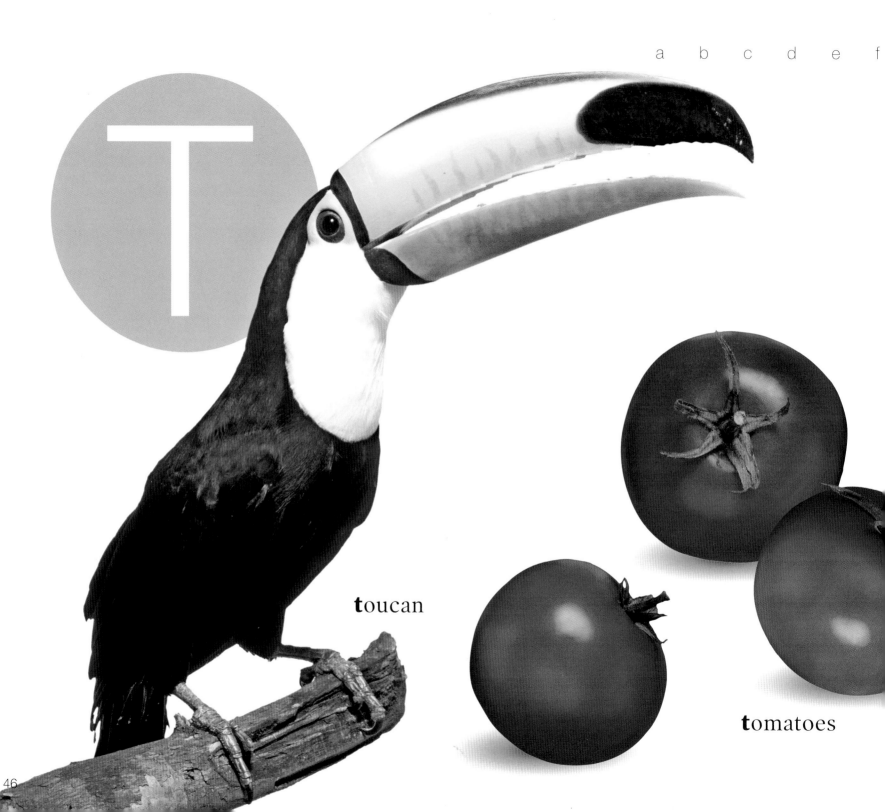

T

toucan

tomatoes

turtle

Two tulips look like a tasty treat
For a turtle who is slow on his feet.
"Don't worry about moving on your tiptoes,
I don't mind sharing the tomatoes."

tulips

The shady green canopy of the umbrella tree,
The universe is a wondrous place to see.
The urchin asks, "Which one's my knee?"

urchin

u u

umbrella tree

The volcano seems subdued.
Vanilla and violets put the vulture in a good mood.
The vampire bat can't take the altitude!

V

vanilla beans

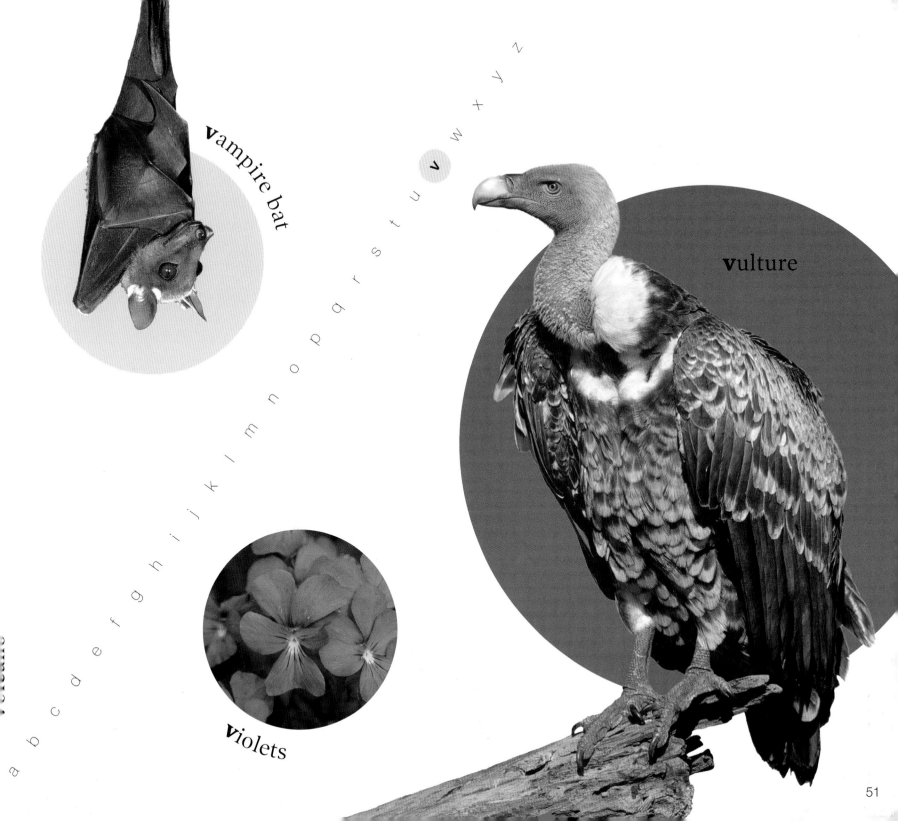

vampire bat

vulture

violets

a b c d e f g h i j k l m n o p q r s t u **v** w x y z

worm

a b c d e f g

walrus

weasel

watermelon

The worm's too slow to wander far
But the walrus is a movie star!
He'll have walnuts and watermelon
at the salad bar.

j k l m n o p q r s t u v w x y z

walnuts

kangaroos

X

puffins

X x

54

chimpanzee

Kiss me!
Don't miss me!
"X" marks the spot,
Pucker up; forget me not.

x
x
x
x

yellow tang fish

Y

Yorkshire terrier

yucca

o p q r s t u v w x y z

yak

Is there a drawback to being a yak?
"Not that I can see; not one setback,
the yams that I eat are a tasty snack!"

yam

ZOÖ

To the zoo!
To the zoo!
The whole crew: the zebra, the lion and
the kangaroo!

zucchini

58

zebra

Acknowledgments:

Play Bac Publishing wishes to thank all the teachers, mothers, and children who have helped develop the eye like® series.

SPECIAL THANKS to: Nadège Michelotto, Ingrid Biraud, Alain Pichlak, Frédéric Michaud, Anne Burrus, Munira Al-Khalili, Elizabeth Van Houten and Paula Manzanero.

All the books in the Play Bac series have been tested by families and teachers and edited and proofread by professionals in the field.

ISBN-13: 978-1-60214-028-8

Play Bac Publishing USA, Inc.
225 Varick Street, New York, NY 10014-4381

Printed in Singapore by TWP

Distributed by
Black Dog & Leventhal Publishers, Inc.
151 West 19th Street, New York, NY 10011

First printing, May 2008

Photography credits:

Meaning of the letters:
h : top ; b : bottom ; d : right ; g : left ; c : center.

BIOS: Alexander M. : 35hd.

CORBIS: Envision : 21hd ; F. Lukasseck : 18c ; TH-Foto : 57bg.

GETTY: Balfour D. : 21c ; Burton J. : 2-C, 2-S, 13c, 45bd, 52g,60hd ; Clayton G. : 39g ; Cole B. : front cover bd, spine, 58hd ; Cordozza T. : 3-N, 34c ; Crawford A. : 44d ; DAJ : front cover c, spine ; Davies and Stars : 15bg, 61 ; Geoff D. : 8-9c ; Gnadinger : 43hd ; Greenaway F. : 43bg ; Hart G.K. & V. : front cover cb, spine, 12c, 47hg, 60 ; Hopkins R.L. : 52-53c ; Kelly J. : 34bd ; Kindersley D. : 2-L, 3-E, 3-F, 6 16-17c, 19c, 30g, 44c, 46d, 58hc, 60hg ; King D. : 2-M, 11bd, 29bg, 32hg ; Laubscher C. : front cover bg, 41d ; McVay R. : 63d ; Massey R. : 3-X, 55bd ; Neunsinger A. : 17g, 30bd ; Ridley T. : 52h ; Rosenfeld M. : 30bd ; Schafer K. : 3-Q, 40h ; Shaff V. : 59 ; Summers K. : 42b ; Taylor K. : 2-S, 45bd, 52g, 60hd ; Teubner 32hg ; Tipling D. : 24c ; Thorsten M. : 54g ; Toon A. & S. : 42-43c, 58bd, ; Vasan G. : 56bd ; Warden J. : 28g ; Weber P. : 5, 31c ; Young J. : 38c ; Zhinong X. : 3-Y, 57bd.

HACHETTE PHOTOS: Arndt I. : 51hg ; Bain K. : 29c ; Bourseiller P. : 50c ; Dressler T. : back cover ; Hamblin M. : 10 ; Heald T. : 22c ; Imagestate : 48 ; Jouan C. : 54-55c ; Jones A. : 25bd ; Martin G. : 27hg ; Mattison C. : 49c ; Rich T.J. : 32d ; Rius J. : 54-55c ; Schanz U. : 27c ; Shah : A. : 55hc ; Thomas F. : 50bg ; Wilde S. : 26bd ;

PHOTONONSTOP: Demotes A. : 33 ; Mauritius : 2-S, 12bd, 45g, 51cd.

SUNSET: Bildarchiv J. : 2-D, 9d, 14c, 20g, 35c ; Delfino : 2-V 51bg ; FLPA : 45c ; GL Production : 2-R, 16b 40-41c, 42hg ; Lacz G. : 37c ; Prix D. : 7h, 18bd ; Oliveira S. : 35bd ; Trompas J.O. : 25hg.

OTHER PHOTOS: DR.

In the same series: